# What's That In The Dark?

**Turn on the light to find the strange night-time creatures. Discover what wildlife creates the peculiar sounds you may hear at night. With illumination turn those hair-raising noises into a moment of discovery. Investigate and learn with light and dark.**

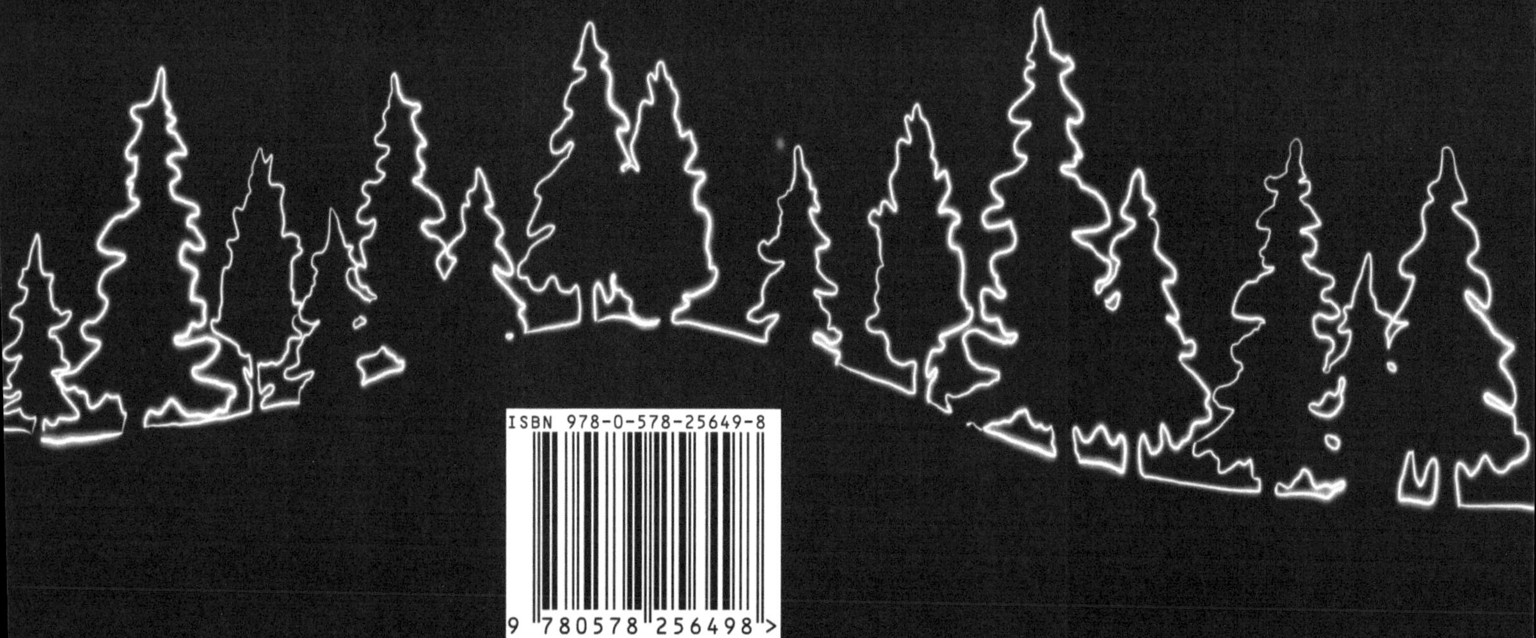

ISBN 978-0-578-25649-8
9 780578 256498 >

# What's That In The Dark?

## Written & illustrated by
## Ann Hoekstra

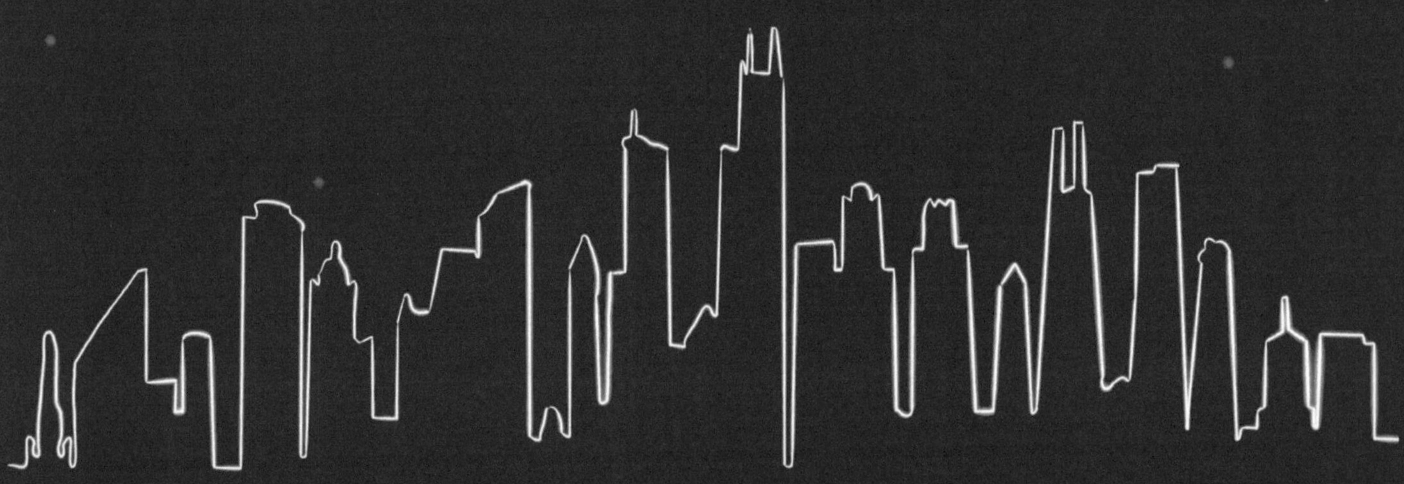

## Copyright October 2021
## Published by Bumples

When it's dark you can't see what's scaring you.

# Turning on the light can make it less scary.

# Fush-fush, what's that?

# It's a moth.

# Scree-scree, what's that?

# It's a screech owl.

# Scritch-scratch, what's that?

# It's a mouse.

# Meow-mew, what's that?

# It's a cat.

# Bark-yip,
# what's that?

# It's a fox.

# Chitter-chee, what's that?

# It's a raccoon.

# Squeak-squee, what's that?

# It's a bat.

# Hiss-zook, what's that?

# It's a possum.

# Scuttle-scurry, what's that?

# It's a cockroach.

# Grunt-urp, what's that?

# It's a deer.

# Smack-grumble, what's that?

# It's a skunk.

# Glug-gurgle, what's that?

# It's a catfish.

# Crikee-chirp,
# what's that?

# It's a cricket.

# Giggle-chuckle, what's that?

Everyone else has left,
what scared them away?

# It's you.

Ann Hoekstra has been awoken more than once by night-time wildlife. In Minnesota, it's always a good idea to have a light on your back porch, and the animals Ann saw inspired her to write this book.

**This book has been created with lots of love and laughter. We would appreciate it if you would leave your review on the link below. We love reading your reviews.**

**Thanks, please leave a review:**

**annhoekstra3@gmail.com**

**bumples2020@gmail.com**

**bumples.com**